instead, it is dark

instead, it is dark

poems

Cynthia Hogue

Red Hen Press | *Pasadena, CA*

Book design by Mark E. Cull

Library of Congress Cataloging-in-Publication Data

Names: Hogue, Cynthia, author.
Title: Instead, it is dark: poems / Cynthia Hogue.
Description: First Edition. | Pasadena, CA: Red Hen Press, [2023]
Identifiers: LCCN 2022028279 (print) | LCCN 2022028280 (ebook) | ISBN
   9781636280653 (paperback) | ISBN 9781636280660 (ebook)
Subjects: LCGFT: Poetry.
Classification: LCC PS3558.O34754 I57 2023 (print) | LCC PS3558.O34754
   (ebook) | DDC 811/.54—dc23
LC record available at https://lccn.loc.gov/2022028279
LC ebook record available at https://lccn.loc.gov/2022028280

The National Endowment for the Arts, the Los Angeles County Arts Commission, the Ahman-
son Foundation, the Dwight Stuart Youth Fund, the Max Factor Family Foundation, the Pasade-
na Tournament of Roses Foundation, the Pasadena Arts & Culture Commission and the City of
Pasadena Cultural Affairs Division, the City of Los Angeles Department of Cultural Affairs, the
Audrey & Sydney Irmas Charitable Foundation, the Kinder Morgan Foundation, the Meta &
George Rosenberg Foundation, the Albert and Elaine Borchard Foundation, the Adams Family
Foundation, the Riordan Foundation, Amazon Literary Partnership, the Sam Francis Founda-
tion, and the Mara W. Breech Foundation partially support Red Hen Press.

First Edition
Published by Red Hen Press
www.redhen.org

Acknowledgments

Thanks to the editors of the following journals for publishing individual poems, sometimes in earlier versions and with other titles:

American Journal of Poetry: "after the war there was nothing"; *Blackbird*: "Regarding Others' Pain"; *Copper Nickel*: "The Underground Village"; *Crazyhorse*: "The Loire Valley (Solstice 2015)," "The Way Is Narrow"; *Cutthroat*: "Bullets Pock the Limestone Walls," "The Understanding," "Witness Triptych"; *The Fiddlehead*: "after the war the house lay in ruins"; *Field*: "To Hide a Child," "Wing (Mary)," "After the War There Was No Food," "The Lost Private"; *Five Points*: "There Never Was a War That Was Not Inward"; *Hinchas de Poesia*: "The Open"; *Hotel Amerika*: "to never complain that the green flecks of leaf offend your view of"; *Interim*: "pavane in five parts"; *Kestrel*: "instead, it is dark," "gift," "Negative," "The River Is Wide"; *Prairie Schooner*: "Flight," "The Mother," "The Opening"; *Shenandoah*: "The Daughter," "The Snake"; *Southern Indiana Review*: "The Father"; and *TAB*: "birdseye," "Then Became."

"The Simple" was a featured poem in the August 2020 issue of *Przekrój*, the oldest cultural magazine in Poland, with an introduction by Julia Fiedorczuk. "After the War There Was Another War" and "The Pacifist" were included in a special issue of *Cutthroat* entitled *Truth to Power: Writers Respond to the Rhetoric of Hate and Fear*, coedited by Pam Uschuk and William Pitt Root. "The Bite of the Apple" was included in the special issue of *About Place* entitled *Dignity as an Endangered Species*, guest-edited by Pam Uschuk. "Author's Note" (published under the title "War Torn") and "the girl on the bridge" were published in a special issue of *Chant de la Sirène* entitled "Poetics, War and Peace," edited by Laura Hinton.

Some lines from "The Open" first appeared in an earlier, uncollected poem entitled "Cardiolesque," published in the journal *Manifest West*.

The title of this collection arrived of itself, apropos of the title poem, but deep in my memory was the title of an exquisite chapbook by the late poet and memoirist Nancy Mairs, *Instead It Is Winter* (The Maguey Press 1977). It took me some time to locate the source of this resonance, but I now can offer thanks and tribute to a great writer and friend: *Nancy, your words stay with me through life.*

Many factors converged to make *instead, it is dark* into a book. Deep thanks to the Anderson Center for Interdisciplinary Studies for the residency fellowship that enabled me to begin seriously writing these poems in a beautiful space (during lilac season no less!). I am grateful as well to the English Department and the Creative Writing

Program at Arizona State University for the leave time that enabled me to research and advance this project. While at ASU, I have had the privilege of meeting and for a time working closely with a number of veterans studying poetry: to Preston Hood, Hugh Martin, and Marco Piña, thank you for your exemplary poetry, and by your example, your generous instruction. Many thanks as well to the friends and colleagues who have helped me in innumerable ways: Wendy Barker, Aliki Barnstone, Elisabeth Frost, Scott Hightower, Laura Hinton, Alan Michael Parker, Alicia Ostriker, William Pitt Root, Pam Uschuk, and Eleanor Wilner. Profound gratitude to Karen Brennan, Christopher Burawa, Martha Collins, Norman Dubie, Elizabyth Hiscox, Joan Larkin, Lois Roma-Deeley, and Lesley Wheeler for timely, crucial reads of this book in progress. And to Kate Gale, Tobi Harper, and Mark Cull of Red Hen Press: I survive as a published poet thanks to you. Always, ever-thanks for the beautiful books you bring into the world, among them, this one.

for Sylvain, life partner and heart's companion

in memory, Stuart Friebert (1931–2020)
writer, seer, mentor, friend

Contents

3. responsibility

4. a love story

instead, it is dark

there, as here, ruin opens
the tomb, the temple; enter,
there as here, there are no doors:
—H.D.

Responsibility is to keep
the ability to respond.
—Robert Duncan

Author's Note

They are called *burned villages*, those towns and hamlets burned to the ground during World War II. There are only a few such villages in France, but when one thinks about any war in history, burned villages are everywhere, embedded in the ground, in the feel, the soil of a place, in a people's living memories and in their stories, at the molecular level in the air we breathe, and in the intensity generated by death and fire—fire power—turning a place where people lived in community together with their animals, their trees and gardens, before soldiers arrived and killed them, into a space where someone can, if she goes to the site, enter the *chora*, "the turbulent surface of the living ground on which or in which every thing is placed, imprinted, while this siting or placement remains always shaken and oscillating in the changes of the becoming." So the philosopher Angus Fletcher describes the Platonic notion of the *chora*, the space bearing the imprint of the things and beings who once lived in that place.

In a time of war, the space people occupy until they can't is war-torn. The *chora* is infused by war's turbulence, which reaches out to disrupt, unsettle, all the delicate integuments of connections at levels both conscious and unconscious—the murmurings and rustlings and burgeonings of lives at levels animal, plant, and mineral—interrupted and changed. What does one see when she visits these sites? Seventy-five years later, the burned village I visited some time ago had been rebuilt, so I could see nothing of the place that had been except via photographs housed in the memorial museum and a documentary shown on the hour, which I happened upon and stayed to watch. In this way, losses in a chronologically distant but spatially proximate war, which had been abstract, historical, were individualized. I found myself feeling for strangers who lost their lives before I was born (as it happens, the year after and in the region where my husband was born). I felt viscerally what it means to "lose one's life," as if I understood that phrase for the first time. Millions upon millions upon millions of people thus.

My skin, my unconscious was also touched—immersed—in the resonance of the violence that had occurred on the site, as if it was a battlefield instead of a place where innocents were slaughtered. I walked through the *chora* on which death was imprinted. I touched a huge larch tree that had survived the fire, still giving shade and respite on a hot summer day. The nerves in my fingertips registered the vibrational frequency of the tree as I ran my hand over its bark. The tree had witnessed the killings. My mind's edges touched the residue this violence had left. Perhaps such residue is what we mean when we say "I feel the spirits of those who died here" when we visit a battlefield, or one of the concentration camps, a site of slaughter. I didn't say anything like that because in this instance I didn't consciously feel anything walking through the rebuilt town, but when I got home, I was violently ill. The condition lasted for days. What I said was, "I don't feel well," but I couldn't articulate the nature of the feeling, that it was a world-sorrow.

1

war's chorus

Witness Triptych

(Paris, 1940)

❧

The bombs starting were mostly mortal
I mean mortar but no one knew that
then. Everyone ran from the house
and somehow we found a deep cave
or grotto and were safe. No one worried
about an occupation. It wasn't real
to us. We caught our breath, listening
for silence, things to go back
as they'd been. Suddenly Mother cried,
Where's the baby where's the baby?
She'd left the baby upstairs and out
she went, gone just like that.

Here I am, I said. Hungry. Not
in the country where we ate well
but couldn't stay, but in the city
which was on rations. Hunger was shadow
was enemy cleaving me. When invaders
knocked like death at our door I answered
for I was small and did not understand
what Father was doing with the archives
records lives he created in the little room
downstairs he called his study. I answered
their questions, told them everything
I thought – why should I not have? – at three
being questioned in a language I didn't speak.

※

What I saw was a huge shadow
with head and hulking back
cast on the wall and looming to ceiling
when Father was arrested.
I was down the hallway from him.
A large man had entered our home,
but I wasn't looking at him but
at the shadow shadow shadow.

To Hide a Child

(France 1941/2012)

1

Who's speaking, please?
It no longer matters.

Who else knew?
No one we trusted no one.

Was the child small enough
to fit in a cupboard?

*One day before soldiers came,
the child* sauvage *arrived*

from the blue horizon, hungry.
Did the child look foreign?

What does foreign
look like to you?

2

How could a child travel alone?
*Not the child but the wild apples
in the fields along the lanes
past our house were our business:*

to collect them in season,
to make the tart sauce
for pork in fall. Did you
hide this child out of guilt?

The child was in danger
from us, unmoved,
gazing out our window.
Did you embellish this story?

3

Children harried, rounded up,
and worse, there, then,
as here, now?

Why not close the blinds
to the soaring poplars, their glossy
leaves and populated shadows?

We happened to be
looking hard and at last
saw that the child's

danger cracking ajar the door
we thought protected us
had let the light in.

The Daughter

(France 1942/2013)

1

I witnessed nothing
to speak of because
we were *Free*.

My life at four was the same
as at three. Then whispers wound
into my ears, or,

Father never whispered –
he gave me fire to breathe –
all the oxygen lit the room,

burning *me* up until my breath
writhed in the body's drum.
Nothing changed but my mind.

2

I have a sense of him having said –
to Mother? a Soldier? –
something, but recall

none of the words,
only a sentence ending,
susurrous, in a hiss,

and I froze. Put together
the words were menacing, sneak-
attacks, after which fear

riddled me day and night
like bullets. I have never not lived
with the fact of having heard,

3

the tear in me trauma
rent when I secreted
zero at the bone.

Father was high up – I never got
his echelon straight before the war
was over – but he was *someone*

who knew things
done to whom by whom
and when I snuck to the door

to listen the sound words
made was lightning flashed
right into my skull.

The Underground Village

There was a village nearby in which everyone herded into the church feared the worst of course they did when an enemy officer was killed but regardless they obeyed as bewildered civilians what else could they do, one bad boy running off and in this way word got out of the church's great doors being barred from outside, the windows too high up to reach, the boy plugging his ears with tears having to hear them and remain hidden and they who bolted the doors, ordered to rough the people in, listened to all they'd wrought until silence fell, charred beams collapsing when tanks shoved walls in. For the rest of the war no one mentioned the neighboring village that had subtracted—disappeared—itself from a ground surface no longer shimmering greenly with safety for one, obeying without questions, but not the other, unasked. Now *not* them. Not soundly. The unheard screams entered their neighbors' dreams, resonants borne by wind, and so, into the vast maze of limestone caves beneath the fields muffling the lowing of the cows corralled below, the singular bark of goats. Above, in the inscrutable farmhouses, old women stirred stone soup in pots over fires they banked, baking an ashen bread. Murderers would arrive by supper.

the girl on the bridge

(France 1944)

a stone bridge to where
                    over what?
the river so low I could've
                    walked across
walked on water walked on water:
it's dark soon, Mother
where she was I didn't know

I was alone wanting to
                    see lights
like fireflies gleaning in the fields at dusk
I was for my age small
                    no one saw me
or the danger they'd have said
I was in but I felt none

what was death to me I
                    hadn't learned
I'd lost my way that was
                    all the scare
I'd ever had until the night sky turned day
I watched in wonder from the bridge
which was in a row with the other bridges

one by one – the aqueduct
                    the rail line
the road across – exploded
                    with loud noise

planes I couldn't see bombs I could as they hit
the whole town different parts lighting up
like a carousel going round and round and round

The Pacifist

War
was
wasteland,
was a way
of putting it.

Loud boombadaboom of the bombs.
Sometimes distant sometimes close.
Each moment asplinter a spark a birth.
Each person a singular globe until
out, out—

No pigs left we did not eat pork.
No cows we did not drink milk.
No chickens we did not boil eggs.

What did we eat I do not remember
eating. Or not eating.

I remember washing maybe once a month maybe once a year.
I wasn't happy or sad neither clean nor unclean.
Mother washing sheets in the stream out back.
Mother selling the rabbit weren't there more we could eat?
Rabbit's dear.

War's a way of living not living.
Question it doesn't matter it's just war always called *the*
just war. I saw through words used to just-
ify war as if glass sharpening sunlight into fire.
I was forever on fire.

instead, it is dark

(1944/2018)

I woke to the dead
and was among them.

how this happened,
who did this to us

unaccountably
hatred glosses

and evidence belies.
ourselves but ourselves.

I'd gone to the corner
when the bakery opened,

mouthing regards
to a rare sun, and then suddenly –

though not – I remember
nothing else.

I feel around me now
and everyone's near

who waited for bread
or God one morning.

it's true I thought at the last
I heard something but didn't think

to turn, nor catch sight of,
nor glean time to.

There Never Was a War That Wasn't Inward

After a line by Marianne Moore

We were free and then we weren't.
Father left for the Front
saying he'd be right back
but he didn't return for years
and then he wasn't himself.

Early June we sat in the garden
sheltered by trees and watched vines
wind up the trellis, each blossom
a melon by August. No one left
knew what to do

when with iron
courtesy the conquerors
speaking their strange tongue
forced open our homes.
At first we didn't know why

we survived when others didn't.
*I can't imagine a world without
me in it*, Mother confessed once,
piercing me because
I could. I had.

We tried "sweetly to go
about our ordinary business"
of being occupied
as with sewing or weeding,
the fight for enough until.

I meant this story to clarify
our quandary. We took care
of ourselves, worried about later,
later. When they left numerously running
we practiced the facts of our innocence.

2

after the war

after the war there was nothing

I did not expect to feel dead
when I died, the cherry around the house
so tall and livid, grave sentinels on the grounds
I walked each day in my mind.

what did you think? you'd asked.
that you were the only one dying?
what language was being
spoken? I was so homesick.

a car arrived among the pungent oak –
"which grow wild as dandelions" –
to take me to a river. still I lay listening,
ants crawling on my face. grass tickled.

I heard a stream burble nearby
and could have wept out loud
for an eternity, seeing how wide
the river was, how far the crossing.

after the war the house lay in ruins

during the war the house fell.
the roof took wing in a hard wind.

now the uncovered walls, open as arms
in supplication to the sky,

herald a ravening
peace – that force in spite

of it all – seeking
the people who'd lived there,

who'd fled, somewhere,
or somehow hadn't, and so,

were stilled with their kith
in a quiet town, the silent night.

After the War There Was No Food

As a boy the man dreamed he lay in a box
of mineral salts, ruby, amber, quartz-clear.

He imagined eating the raw meat
of the goat whose milk he sucked as newborn.

Death was his mother, match-thin
and unsmiling. He loved her fiercely,

voraciously
bleating into her sad face as he nursed.

Starving, the boy grew tall but not straight,
so lean the wind might sweep him off.

Lately, the man returned to the Forêt de Chinon,
which did not comfort him,

so many trees harvested
he lost his way. Hunger

was all he'd known when
a long time ago he pleaded

for Death his mother
to feed him. He bent to touch

himself because, after all,
Death would not.

Flight

Years later the once-child would recount almost casually how many experiments the enemy performed on the angel, whom she called *Father*, when the angel was a POW. Because he was fallen, they cut him without anesthesia to see if it hurt. They removed an insignificant organ—then a significant one—to see if the etheric angel-body could heal itself. They debated removing his wings. Some of them wanted to make him fly first but they feared he'd escape. One came to him in pain, seeking absolution. *My soul to keep*, the man whispered furtively, but also a bit frantically. *Fate's upon us*, he cried. The angel found language fled. The once-child had told the story many times of her father's return, how he'd been arrested a soldier but returned an angel, silent and scarred. How then the angel had left the once-child's mother and how poor they were. The once-child hadn't mentioned that Father'd been tortured until the cousins' meal, as if silence erased trauma, and the angel always gone for good.

Bullets Pock the Limestone Walls

Late in life the Teacher was asked what the Occupation was like. He'd still taught the village children math and history as if the world weren't at war, and they'd behaved or misbehaved and he'd rapped knuckles hard or else the children wouldn't listen and everyone was hungry but they all bit down and did what they had to because, *unfortunately, we had to.* He'd never mentioned the forced walks along the railroad tracks that brought arms and supplies to the front and prisoners away, the daily orders to scout for wires tucked under the ties by the Resistance, which he'd hoped to help by not seeing what he saw. Hope is the thing that fetters. If he found nothing what harm in following orders? He would survive. The Occupiers did not belong there though they acted as if they owned everything, the village and the villagers, and when they barked *Do it* everyone always did. What was it like? *No different*, he said. *We weren't affected.* Maybe he believed himself that moment he was asked the prying question as he sat on the plastic veranda he'd built when he retired, where the sun shone and the stray came to beg and the tarragon and wild strawberries grew alongside. Tomorrow he'd spend all morning picking them they were so small and ripe.

The Mother

(France ca. 1950)

Scrubbing sheets in the stream in winter. Subtracts herself from the brittle grass, cement porch of the laundry house where women work Saturdays, and from the others to— "forbid it Lord"—somewhere beyond the ken of claims to certain rights, the law that doesn't ask what it feels like to coincide with another, to be in the space of *encounter.* The law that asks how we are "to understand that which differs from our capacity" to understand. Is it Cartesian to ask why she's not the rabbit she knows lives off their garden, who never has to wash the winter linen? She doesn't know this rabbit. The sheets freeze as they dry in ripples patterned by a bitter wind. Adds herself to the equation, what she bears witness to.

The Father

It's true he kicked the boy when
he was too squeamish to hook a worm
but not very hard.

He might have launched his son
into the water though the father planted
the kick on impulse,

it meant nothing
but *I am the ruler of your
world*. Swiftly executed.

The boy, who hadn't expected it
nevertheless knew his father and
kicked himself for standing too close.

I'm so stupid, he thought,
which he said aloud as tonight
after dinner the story –

so long at the bottom of memory's lake –
surfaced, bloated, eyes eaten away,
the thing he'd hooked at last.

The man held up the catch, seeing how
small the tyrant had been, cowed
into outbursts since the Liberation,

a passivist saying when asked,
No, we were not touched
by the war. We were not curious.

Surviving, his father found kindness
sheened with cruelty like armor,
which is what sank, rusted away.

The Opening

Rare the fish the boy
               found streamside
when he first devised the game –
look for the narrowest place
to cross the creek to build a dam –
gather the leaves
               from forest floor,
twigs and branches
               to bolster the frame,
grow the structure until
he'd created a cascade
in miniature or salmon ladder
for a tiny salmon to swim home.

Water works its way around.
               Father made him
throw a sunfish back.
They happened on the entrance to
the cave in a hillock upstream
so overgrown they must have
               missed it many
times. Inside was nothing
               but the barest trace –
two lines to sketch a something's
horns, a curve for hump. A partial
something else beneath the chalky
lichen, but enough to realize everywhere

the evidence of ancient hand –
and modern when the boy broke
a stalagmite, the top he pocketed.
They never spoke of how
                    they'd stumbled
onto a vast silence, how gamely
                    they had crawled
into a hillside opening to nowhere
anyone knew to be significant, and faced
the darkness no light breached before,
and corridors of void like empty arms.

After the War There Was Another War

The man's cousin, six years older when drafted
to Algeria, *saw things*, they said,
the war being fought by then *with gloves off.*

                    How history's
trace resides in a country's language.
fifty years later, the cousin gasping for breath,

the man understood that all the white
wine, harsh and constant cigarettes
were also a language,
                that his cousin's other-
worldly laughter welled from an ancient memory
of having once *belly* laughed.

Like riding a bike, they said. Time heals
nothing. Defeated, the colonizers created
for their children a doctored history.
When conscripted, the man whiled his time
cleaning the rifle he still keeps in the upper closet,
                    oiled and ready.

3

responsibility

birdseye

swirl of flock,
sky black with

                hundreds: a whole
                murder of crows?

Who among us knows
      the root in battles'

                corpse-fields,
                wraith of once-seen

raven parliaments?
We, who merely

                watch
                    bird-whirl
                        spiraling
                            down as
                    one to
                earth not
              dirt
but asphalt
tennis courts

                replacing wetlands,
                do not.

I'm startled by the caws of laughter
seeing crows persist

in gathering at anciently
the *mere*,

which was, edged in rue,
somewhere here.

memory holds a trace that at times rises into words

. . . we could try to console ourselves with the thought
that there was nothing we could do . . .
—Malcolm Gladwell

That first time Columbine I was a producer
never a reporter so I wasn't sent right away and
believe me it was a relief not to have to cover that
blood not to film them

close up cleaning up but they sent me the next week
for the funerals and all those bodies those young
faces because every casket you know was open
every single one and what I

what I had to make sure was covered   was –

I'm sorry I sound upset but I'm

not really it's that reporting the news

what's the news since cable

now what's news called news isn't –

the week after the shootings was the closing
of each lid on each child so many shuttered lids we
had to record each shutting out the child's light and
, the

luckily with this latest I'd taken the week off so I
didn't have to go but we're covering the funerals

now you saw that right?
but I've stopped producing so I didn't have to

I'm not crying but when

you've seen so much the miles

of raw footage we filmed and had to cut and

watch over and over to edit you

don't forget

Regarding Others' Pain

Something becomes real—to those who are elsewhere,
following it as "news"—by being photographed.
—Susan Sontag

1

She sat on the windowsill
    one leg thrown over the green sash
        like riding a horse.

The men in the room talked
    quietly. She ignored them,
        watching a car slow,

the driver leering at her bare leg
    and bumping the curb.
        He was a doctor or something,

doffing his hat to her neighbor in curlers
    on the porch in her nightie.
        Mornings the grackles were loud,

and the men grew loud as they spoke
    of a burgeoning civil war
        and what should be done.

They were all white, and argued
    as if the force of their words
        had a power they might activate,

2

driving a solution no one anywhere
      imagined. They did not think
            about how they sounded.

So full of, she thought, *confidence* –
      maybe not her forte –
            holding the belief

that words mattered was ir-
      resistable when they got
            going. She'd never before

not believed them. Now they
      couldn't agree. She'd seen
            the pictures of those

thousands insistently refused
      refuge, insisting; and observed
            how in telling daily

moments the simple
      small cruelties proved all-
            but imperceptibly tempting,

3

the gentle maneuver of with-
        holding something, the
                kindly (so it seemed)

delivery of *no*, the half-
        smile of regret, like a door
                shown, after which,

the cutting the person
        cold to shame, to
                show them who had

the power, or that when one –
        calling himself a leader –
                yelled *out out out*

he meant business. Then
        people hopped to expel
                the outsider whose

mouth – as the crowd
        pushed with its pincered
                mind – was a perfect O.

gift

to receive a scare isn't
to cut someone whether with words
or a kitchen knife, a fist
that knocked through drywall
                and not my face . . .

that started small and at first –
teasing about looks, the
demeaning nicknames –
bared teeth of smile:
                but you did not kill me,

I think of L who
dowered with whole heart
pain to "teach me" –
could and could
but did not (never listened)

so it deepened,
violence delivered
like a bouquet
to my door –
                kabloom!

I packed my nightmares,
got out forever
I vowed until soft soft
nothings on the phone
where I lived alone

among concrete blocks,
orange shag rug (very
cheap and very mine
and very very fine)
when he found me again:

don't you ever

                          ever . . .

heaving I was heaving
breathing though I did not
crack like *the other*:

this memory's a trick of
thought I thought,
remembering – was lucent gift,
a potion I gulped – desperately
swallowing, unforgetting

The Bite of the Apple

1

In the backyard the apple tree had a dignity the child never thought twice about I mean why would she question what was always a given? It was tall—and spreading—shaded the whole yard, its fruit sweet and freely she ate and freely climbed. From the highest bough she could reach the garage roof in one direction and in the other her sister's upstairs nursery. If she stretched she might touch the window's glass like God or fall like Lucifer. Years later the girl biked with her sister to an orchard to pick apples as it happened for the last time they felt at ease in their bodies untouched by power. Soaring past waving fields, they glowed in the lucent fall. Small were the clouds the golden cumulus that day but firm their place in the wider sky.

2

Like the cumulus the small woman however touched as a girl by power affirmed herself before a wide congress of stares in the name of truth though accused of accusing one of the Elect, himself when before the tribunal sneering in outrage I'm sure sincerely after all no other woman had dared name him but she from his own class and race and save for gender the privilege he'd been born into which is to say for her a more provisional version. She'd harmed him he said for good. *I liked beer I still like beer* he repeated to make a point he seemed to think clear. The woman accused of accusing spoke softly in a high voice because she was she said afraid to speak up, but her words made evident the strength no one had bent, the dignity none could tar. The woman had in essence picked the apple the man then asserted for himself. His alone to eat. Thereafter would he abide himself as an apple abides the mouth. The seeds of the core the teeth.

Negative

1

The moon glints off
a third-floor window when you near

the house in the glen
on top of a small, wooded rise.

You cry *Help*, faintly,
a word you don't like, a limited word

when you mean something
deeper that gestures toward root cause

and cure, the way *seed* in other languages
signifies all stages of growth.

2

Think of a circle, a labyrinth,
think of wholeness,

how the door's handle's being held
by a woman gesturing for you

to follow her past stairwells
and alcoves, a hospital,

until at last looms the library:
floor to ceiling shelves

of leather-bound books so much
to learn in no-time,

3

in no-time so much to do.
How to approach such knowing?

Language rooted in earth – like plants –
when sounded opens the mind's portals.

The woman says almost casually
You weren't chosen: remember?

You mumble *help* again,
adding *me* this time, in that instant

understanding she'd give her life
if it'd make up for anything,

4

anything at all though you don't know
what the woman – who now rests her arm

over the shoulder of a man
taking his glasses off,

his swollen eyes, rolling tears,
the reddened skin of his brow

where veins pulse beneath
like a system of streams

in the negative of an aerial photo
you can't look away from – regrets.

Wing (Mary)

You hear *Magdalenë Magdalenë*. You thought yourself alone here. It's not your name but you answer regardless. Sap trickles from breast and thighs. Trees sweat, gray and hard as a hound's call, the forest thickly wooded.

When there's no room left, you scrawl names with the branches of trees, which splinter in cold. In a clearing you make angels, arms and legs working. Halos wings gowns in a sweep.

The lake is icy and safe for the moment, the ice hulking along shore, bordering the white hillside. *This is how it always was.* Call it an unreadable pattern, all those melting tracks uncovering the random strips of green beneath. Or wing it.

pavane in five parts

.

1

what happens to you happens to us all

you can change some things but mostly you can't
change others have you tried of late? of late I see
signs you're holding something back, or in – how do
you say that? – but you know what I mean. quickly,
what is it you felt you wanted to *tell* me? if you know
what, what?

2

after a rape (for D.B.)

fractures the person you were after which
there's no ~~you~~. forget to converse. waking confuse
name. sever sometime hence: spirits
                                    come in dreams – talk
in spells. words you don't know if they speak to or
cure you. I say *I'm uncomfortable feeling for
you*. mend may. beneath integument the cord of
                                    you holds.

3

the trial is not a trial

appeals are evaluated according to the criteria here's a list. your new evidence will be forwarded for reconsideration. we claim to be as clear as day though we'll never explain how we came to our decision only that we're always right: here are the directions which are ambiguous please follow them to the letter.

4

déjeuner sur l'herbe

the table along the river was set for the family to
gather at the *guinguette* everyone would be there the
cousins on the poor side and the in-laws who had the
business and were rather well off and offered to pay
for everything though no one had asked but everyone
ohed and *ahed* when the in-laws took the bill &
insisted as if the sum was nothing to them they'd
hardly notice. his wife's bracelets were there but she
wasn't. an odd absence no one mentioned. ill
already? you wondered later about she who would
though no one knew yet not see the new year. she had
called jauntily after him as he left—*I'll be with you
all in spirit*—and then lay back on the couch to read
Camus because for some reason she couldn't explain
she needed something from language on fire with
truth.

5

pavane pour les enfants défunts

among the scattering of lives after violence & minds suddenly unfettered. a hundred thousand dust-to-dust particles to companion but not to accompany. to mourn them all alone each child black white brown because we can't talk reason or stop them yet—the Loaded Guns—& stand guard: what I mean is that earthbound we bear the souls departed in open arms which empty & overhead the dun uplift of so many wings.

The River Is Wide

The stretch of
> gray water, bordered by
> algae near the riverbank,

a speckly green path,
patches the size of my foot, stepping stones,
and as slippery,
> a surface I wouldn't break,
> all the icky fish, crayfish, catfish,

teeming underneath, nibbling bubbles.
The river could feed an army.

I was an army of one.
> Skinny arms and bobbing head:
> fighting form (in my mind).

I could walk on water
(in my dreams).
When I spoke,
> my thoughts pushed
> the moist air like reality

I might change.
Swayed by the power I felt,

I'd board a ferry
             to cross the Red River
             and staunch the blood.
On the other side, I think,
I'll try a staying hand on the arm
raising the gun,
             a laying on of hands
             to heal spirit. False god,
you cannot heal someone of mortal wounds
or change that one who killed.

For him the *I*'s not real. Judgment
             shall find him
             wanting. I was invisible.
Silenced. That I held my tongue
(did I put it down with my courage?).
I'd say the ferry of grace
             sank, that I stepped off the prow
             to swim, thinking to reach
the willows and sycamore aflutter
like hands on shore. Maybe waving.

The Simple

The women cluster at the cathedral,
hair in careful bouffant helmets,
armored and elegant, poised to herd
                              purposefully
                              into Mystery.
I want to do that too, but then tear up I can't
                              say why.

Stand still. Wind wisps my hair that gently
you brush like stardust from my eyes. Light shifts
and colors sharpen. Across the square the Grand
                              Hotel sparkles with
                              chandeliers, mirrors
upon mirrors in gold-leaf frames: the soaring empty space
                              of the Symbolic.

Throngs pass in and out of these yawning
doors, the alacritous doormen, the language
of bodies feeling fear, love, pain – desire –
                              equitably: a gift
                              of insight
we hadn't asked for or realized we'd received,
                              a simple,

an edge of the Negative: *not* simple
but potent, to refuse absolutes, remain
in process, healing the (my) emotional
                                    body in order
                                    to keep open
the possible. The huddling women who'd seemed
                                    so done up

are wounded, not *not* beautiful,
as in the strength with which they clutch one
another, eloquent now their faces have character,
                                    expressed in
                                    the parlance
of style we could read but not speak, always our
                                    broken word.

4

a love story

Love,
The door opens, you walk in.
— Muriel Rukeyser

"then became"

Smog-dust
lusters into
        wing-gift with you

This glistening fractal = =
the actual pattern of Love = =
        our *granted*

and fragile bower
in which = = greenly, our One's = =
        bestowed

The Open

("in which every being is freed")
after Rilke

❦

To not reach = = my arms ex-

tending, emptied = =
     you soared
          away

to die, then be re-

vived. One second
     I was bringing
          you coffee,

then erupted / pain took = = you

would not talk just dis-
     appeared into = =
          I tried calling

you back = = as you left everything.

❧

I followed the distant siren,

flashing light,
        abruptly shorn /
                of you: in mortal

danger, you the subject of my (loss

of) faith that we for-
        ever could companion,
                alone together = = I now en-

trusted to the scattering of = =

꿏

Chance: you left for ER /

you did not
= = stop for Death = =
        Your first words:

If I had died I'd be at peace.

What could I say?
        After great pain,
                the feet like

stone don't lift, then the letting-go?

But you didn't.
        Storms sun-struck
                spun like gold birds

when Hope forthwith furled:

the necessary angle of mind
        instantly to un-
                fetter

The Snake

We thought it squashed, a spotty
                tan tube on dusty
                asphalt. Still
undulate of S –
"crushed by the grinding weight
of superstition" –
                unspooled from
                a sheltering bush
along the ditch, camouflaged,
noticed just in time.

In the distance mountains
                dipped in clouds.
                Somewhere east
it rained. Staying me,
in "the natural order of things
unimaginably vast and complex,"
                you stoned the snake.
                Bad luck, I cried.
I didn't know
I thought that, but felt it as stone

after stone whistled straight
                on target,
                understanding being
one of humans' most austere
of pleasures: Not killing, no,

nothing so absolute;
               curiosity more like it,
               the inexplicable having
occurred: at the last moment each stone
swerved eerily off in parabolic arcs,

as if freed from some terrible purpose
               by an orb of protection
               we couldn't see
shielding the snake.
Anyway, you said, turning,
throwing a last shot, *it's dead*.
               But I was lured
               to look back,
blink as stone veered,
snake braided and was gone.

The Lost Private

The desk chair on the mountaintop
that the man once found facing the valley

looked too rickety to sit on.
He saw it suddenly from the steep trail

most hikers never took. Not him,
who went off trail every chance he had,

even sometimes losing his way.
Beside the chair lay a blue plastic bag

with identification card (listing an address
on a military base closed fifteen years ago),

mold-covered prison release papers,
a suicide prevention plan (writing washed off),

and Deputy Majeho's legible local phone number
writ large. Parole Officer.

This morning the man leafs through the papers
when a ragged scrap flutters out:

the same neat hand made a note,
Cheryl   573-[unreadable, unreadable, torn away].

Whether and when something was done
or undone the man cannot say –

for years he'd forgotten about the unknowable –
but what he feels among the mold-dust

he breathes in reading the documents
for signs of a lost life

is an indifference to the broken
heart of himself who now alone

could not for the life of
him walk that mountain.

to never complain that the green
flecks of leaf offend your view of

1

the horizon above cloud layer when you glimpse the
huge reddening and almost flattening-out sun that
deepens your reserve in the moment

> introducing an end time
> to such beauty amidst which

you'd been thinking about something else   if you
think about *it* (instead of merely tearing up) you'll
in the end get around to the fact of it though

> such talk suggests defeat
> or maybe resignation

2

but definitely not something anyone would want to
feel I mean do you?
of course that's quite unfair of me!   you've been
so steadfast kind

> who've had so much
> to lose –

and so much lost – a city once, and not so long ago,
the three-hundred-year-old farmhouse on its outskirts you'd
restored   I've called the tendency

      by others whom you've
      loved to clean you out

3

"disinheritance," but you don't call it anything less
than *luck* because you always never minded, said,
standing stalwart as the large elm

      where beneath you found
      as if you hadn't ever looked

before your voice among the morel, *All that stuff's
immaterial*: the sudden overwhelming scents of lilac
and crabapple that you're about to take the time

      to follow like a cardinal
      direction after all

The Way Is Narrow

On the cathedral the middle portal is Judgment
(say Discernment).
The last is Grace.
She commands (Attention) with her scepter,
fashions Herself as offering (Law). *But who am I*
                    to judge? Lines of visitors,

queuing to pass through Grace's doors,
convolute through the square,
chatting and secular.
The river flows hard, boats churning today.
Wind takes my hat. I run into a wedding
                    portrait, which I ruin.

Who's the stranger
with her arms grasping
as if in Desire?
A chic couple cuts in the line ahead of a child
who dodges in front, whirling around,
                    a Fury chastising them. Suddenly,

we're audience to a Morality play: Shame
shadows the cheeky pair
when they try, intrepid,
to move further up. It costs nothing to wait your turn
to enter, your soul to leave through the first portal,
                    empty, and emptyhanded.

The Understanding

1

An invitation from the aged industrialist
you knew only through your ex's family

surprised us, that it included me.
I'd met no one from your old set –

the swinging 68ers – because
they'd dropped you. Here, the signs

of welcome were unmistakable:
Oysters on the settee arranged in

their nacreous shells (though out of season,
milky as dead cow eyes),

sauce a light vinegar flecked
with translucent bits of onion

the host made clear he'd chopped.
Three-pronged forks, lemon wedge. Champagne –

the color of corn silk after shucking corn –
so chilled it effervesced into the nose.

We floated to a table set with bone-
china, ivory linen cloth, and crystal glass.

2

The wine with dinner tasted of old shoes,
and dribbled leather slivers down our throats.

The industrialist waited for your judgment.
You, considered, adroit: "One can taste that

it *was* a good wine," and he, "I brought it
from the *cave* for you, a '43, but sadly

kept too long." Was the vintage –
your birth year – accidental?

I wondered in my awful nosiness. No,
simply "the best of wartime vintages,"

so easy to procure in town where Occupiers
lived it up. Yes, he'd continued to do business,

no need to flee when *business was so good*.
They'd bought what he made, paid on time,

left him alone, though he'd been careful
in his words, all cultured surface, *cloisonné*.

They'd never guessed his thoughts.
He tipped his head in an old habit:

still he watched his words. Would
we like sorbet to cleanse the palate?

3

I understand only at the moment
this morning when I read in *Little Saint*

how in June 1940 as the invading force
reached town, "It was frightful,

oh the war broke all our lives,"
that those products, the screws or ball-

bearings, the things that were so useful
in the War, made for machines now

obsolete, were means the industrialist had;
that memories stored in a cool, dark place

can turn to dregs though
kept at constant temperature;

and we had tasted something which
nothing in years since could cleanse.

The Loire Valley (Solstice 2015)

The uncoursed sun, a vulnerable
$\qquad\qquad$ evening's chords
$\qquad$ of fallow field,
the mounded rows you think at first are graves,
which we traverse to reach
$\qquad\qquad$ the one-thousand-year-old
$\qquad$ fortified grange.

Somehow it missed the war though everything
$\qquad\qquad$ near the railroad's
$\qquad$ gone to bits.
Nothing in this place to fix or modernize.
No one to claim it. Someone's vision
$\qquad$ was to fill
$\qquad$ the vaulting barn

once a year with music around now.
$\qquad\qquad$ Silence opens wooden gates
$\qquad\qquad$ made from the primeval forest
cleared to farm. The pockmarked limestone walls
enclose a cluttered courtyard
$\qquad\qquad$ in the middle of which
$\qquad\qquad$ humans mill, perusing

cd's, having drinks among the cattle stalls.
$\qquad\qquad$ Inside is Bach,
$\qquad\qquad$ and tonight an owl

whose contrapuntal hoots
you hear before you see him

> land high in the rafters just
> like your dream of flying.

At midnight, sun dipped down at last,

> the full moon
> floodlights the watch tower.

The gates closing, we're cast out
to the carless field, nor other farmstead near

> to dim the sense of
> not belonging here.

Notes

Some years ago, coinciding to the *hour* of my breaking a long writing hiatus, my husband had a massive heart attack. The first poem I wrote thereafter, while he was still in the ICU, was based on a dream that he, born during WWII in occupied France, had as a child growing up in a time of vast postwar food shortages. Blurring the boundaries between fact and truth, the poem drew on this recounting of a memorable dream that my husband had told me several times over the decade of our marriage. I had not realized I'd been listening so hard when he shared such a memory of an era and a place more than half a century and half a world away from my own childhood in the plenty of postwar America.

In this unexpected way, I embarked on a path to discover if there were more such memories in the extended family in France, harbored so deeply those remembering didn't even know it until someone—a curious American— asked them. Abiding love, humble thanks, and, in some cases, tribute to those who have shared memories that infuse these poems: Monique and Guy Ardré, Michel and Annick Cocard, Inge Cocard, Marie-Annick Fraisse, Roger and Lily Gallais, René and Madeleine Gallais, Louis and Mado Maupetit. Great thanks to Dr. Susan Fischer, who hosted a tea in order that I might interview Laurence Doubinsky, who so generously spoke with me for more than an hour about her early memories of the war, and especially of her father, who was in the Resistance in Paris. And finally all, everything, to Sylvain Gallais, *without whom nothing*.

war's chorus

"To Hide a Child": The poem draws loosely on details recounted in *Village of Secrets: Defying the Nazis in Vichy France*, by Caroline Moorehead.

"The Pacifist": Some words in the poem drawn from *Joan Darc*, the English translation of Nathalie Quintane's French original, *Jeanne Darc*, translated by Sylvain Gallais and Cynthia Hogue.

"There Never Was a War That Was Not Inward": (Mis)quoted line and some general facts drawn from Robert Gildea's *Marianne in Chains: Daily Life in the Heart of France During the German Occupation*.

after the war

"The Mother": Quoted lines from Emily Dickinson and (slightly misquoted) Ron Broglio's *Surface Encounters: Thinking with Animals and Art*.

"After the War There Was Another War": The second italicized phrase is a translation of how de Gaulle once described the brutal French policy during the Algerian War of Liberation. The poem's closing lines were inspired by Hugh Martin's poem, "M-16A2 Assault Rifle" from *The Stick Soldiers*.

responsibility

"memory holds a trace that at times rises into words": The text of this poem has its origins in a deeply moving phone conversation with my sister, an ABC News producer, Elaine Hogue, recalling the trauma of covering Columbine (1999) at a time when she was off duty and therefore did not have to cover the San Bernadino massacre (2015). Quoted with permission.

"pavane in five parts": Part two is for Devereaux Baker; part five memorializes the Tucson shooting (2011), the Sandy Hook Elementary School shooting (2012), and the Marjory Stoneman Douglas High School shooting (2018).

"The Simple" is for poet and Joyce scholar, Brian Caraher.